VOLCANO

ELOSHAM VOG

PREFACE

Seven Lucky Gods

A plaster clock,
brass-girdled.

The old man,
glasses an open film can.

A face mounted on a machine,
hand-cranked slowly like a cigarette's flicker.

Dumbo, fat,
cheeks sparked with mirth.

Open bottles.

Nature in her infinite wisdom,
close up a corkscrew of penis and hair.

A silent comedy of elsewhere.

VOLCANO

✤ DRAMATIS PERSONAE ✤

```
F…...................Woman
HIM…..............All Men
TROJANS..........Hungry Spirits
CHORUS………...The Birds   .
```

✤ SCENE ✤

Ancient Greece, contemporary Hawai'i,
and the British Isles at all points in time

I

CHORUS: A VOLCANIC HISTORY, PART IV

Superstition

Socrates invented the ghosts
in these islands, a non-believer,
eyes ignited with a tale:

Night, his pipe gone out, echoes of rain
through gutters, wind a forsaken sound
superfluous as tears.

The house empty. A knock,

his dead father at the door,
Windsor knot loosened, face undone,
wilted prayer in his eyes.

Socrates stood. He stared.

His father screamed through silence,
lips turning purple, fingers lifted
in benediction or warning.

Socrates knelt before his father
the spirit and bowed his head.
The volcano floated within.

Auspices of Transience

He is a refugee from the city of hash and twigs.
The suitcase he carries is half-empty.
She was grown in a glasshouse fueled by brimstone and burnt words.
The ancient heat warms her back from afar.

He rubs coconut oil into callus each time he rests.
His scarred soles show routes traced through ash and sand.
His path leads to the last fringe of trees to circle the earth.

She drifts past buoyed by a salted breeze.
Her limbs trail dry tendrils of root that cry hymns to the sky.
Her vertebrae bear faded anchors in blue.

In the green shadow of banyans his inertia recedes.
Her joints are pomegranate seeds popping.
Time stops as eyes meet under the watchful gaze of the birds.

(*Stage directions:* Pan right, past doors
of houses left ajar, past fragments of voice
and light cast through cracks, past scrapes
silvering into scars, past waves crashing
onto sand formed from shell and stone
and the coral bones of the island.

Pause.

Cut to a tableau of standard domesticity
with a garden theme, masses of leaves
and blossoms bright against the fade.)

Cold Night with Wild Turkey

He sipped at his second-rate malt, temple
bells ringing out across the dark graveyard.

This was it—but it couldn't be, not this
sad imitation of a love-filled life.

He turned to haiku, built stilted houses
to hold history safe above the flood

of tears and fear, not a single garden
plot free from budding plumeria trees.

The volcano grew. Pickled synapses
snapped the chains of classics—man grown arcane,

ancient flag out of reach on the moon like
pyramids built by aliens on earth.

He'd mistaken the electric toaster
for good fortune, x-rays for intelligence,

hairspray and surfboard resin for happiness—
misinterpretations of maladies

his new literature of modern love.

CHORUS: A VOLCANIC HISTORY, PART III

Resonance

In the mirror stood his father,
fingers stroking the oversized buckle of the belt
whose whistle formed the backing track
to night in the city of hash and twigs.

Sneer clamped around his pipe, eyes lit
by some internal fire, he snorted
as he spoke his final words: *A creature
like you—you'll never keep a woman.*

Independence Day
or Ladies' Night at The Trojan

He sat alone, thinking of F
with her friends, glass of whisky
a solace, the sky splitting
with slivers of light.

He turned westward
from the garden, wandered
half-lit streets to the graveyard
where he knew they'd be:

Lovers unlocked at night, love
nothing more than breath
among pitted wings streaked
with white, silhouetted angels

circling in the dark. The watching birds
leaned closer.

Pornography

In a dark corner, Lenin listens to the people and nurses his drink.
The brown bottle proletariat call him over to show him their dreams.

   The woman, shopworn, roots for truffles.
   The dog drags closer, small brain fearing
   castration. She strokes his suspicions.
      Look. The camera is stark, raw.
      She stares straight into the lens.
   He whimpers, unburdened, transfixed by
   the corkscrew. Above, Jesus exposes
   his sacred heart, red lava wriggling
   to the dictates of ancestral heat.
   The prey clings to his woman.

Unnoticed amid laughter, Lenin picks up his book and mendicant's
        bowl.
He turns and climbs worn cement stairs to frosted fields waiting under
        the moon.
Shirtless, he kneels in mud and strikes his back with handfuls of hard
        barley pods.

He does it again.

CHORUS: A VOLCANIC HISTORY, PART II

Homecoming

Father sat in his armchair,
tapping a pipe with briar eyes,
papers in the ashtray black.

His splayed hands molded a cherry
which glowed condemnation
against penitent skin, dropping live sparks,

imprinting a judgment passed
through a mouthful of sulfur and ash
and remorseless old age.

Time to think! The pipe moved,
embers a promise. Father's eyes did not.
His hands toxic thereafter.

Post-Coital Depression

Making love, he cried
when he climaxed.
Neighbor dogs howled.
The earth shook with laughter,
happy with her other lovers.

CHORUS

Bullet

- My parents were married, a terrible thing.
  A life of love, sex, work, labor-saving
  appliances and routine dental hygiene.

- Is that why you're still single?

A Critical Analysis of Misbegotten Love

Witness the facsimile unfolding before the banyan:

F oscillating under rainclouds, her reflection streaked
like stalks of red ginger. The man crisp, eyes a creased roadmap
concealing his loss. He walks with no apology.
She is struck by his self-possession.

F transmits unbound electrons with her eyelids,
playful, to the tune of the attraction of opposites. He records
his days, asleep. Foreign films accent the crossing of her legs,
sticky like a blood clot plucked with lacquered nails, the effect
highlighted by her failure to see:

Tiresias, frozen in time, a halved man who tipped his cap,
tapped his cane, and vanished
into the shadow of silver ions stolen from the earth,
his mind filled with the keen of birdsong.

Now, wild idea to unravel the patriarch's riddle:
he'd propose. What if—

Stop, he ordered himself. *The visionary wings spoke of other things.*

In Which He Reconceives Himself as a Martyr

Ragged silence greeted F, his breath
tripping from the receiver into her kitchen—
dark, robust. He didn't know what to say.

Fear seemed vulgar as jazz, suspicion
nothing but a banana leaf to conceal
his nakedness. She sighed

and he imagined her eyes
pulling him down like dark water. Jesus,
haunted by prayer and romantic poetry

stitched together by ghosts, felt
the angry fever rise, the clamor
of female spirits suffocating his dreams.

He surrendered without honor,
understanding F was forever inscribed
in eyeliner across his sweat-soaked soles.

The operator laughed as he ended the call.

CHORUS: A VOLCANIC HISTORY, PART I

Locker Room

Four dark shadows.
A fist.
A doorway
  held open.
One drunk trespasser
  plus a hoarse laugh
  echoing from concrete.
A garnish of hope:
  his clenched hands,
  useless, swinging
  left and right.
A graffiti of sound.

(Deep down, he knows
this was not the beginning.)

Metamorphosis

In the beginning, her lizard skin was supple, didn't flake
into island-shaped sheets drifting on wind.
Her long tongue stayed curled behind neatly filed teeth.

In the beginning, her face was empty, wrinkles unearthed
beneath pound shop rouge and borrowed skin. Her blood
was warmed by the presence of him.

In the beginning, her eyes reflected his lies
instead of other men. Her clawed fingers flexed
around flowers and fine wineglass stems.

In the beginning, the world was silent.
The telephone lay dormant, waiting.

volcano

kneeling in thick red loam
heaving, shoulders hunched,
he, reluctant lover ostracized
by love, feels the bile rise in his
throat worn raw from screaming,

his eyes closed tight on the
orange rush of dawn in the jungle
around him. his father's words buzz
in his brain, the fights with F
the backbeat to this day, here

and now. and now he tenses,
clenches tobacco-stained fingers
against steel-blue gun
and kowtows in a snakelike
contortion, mouth opened wide.

through him rushes history,
dark nights happy and sad,
half-dissolved days spent
building this rainbow of ochre
and green, glitter-burnt stars

and steam. and he waits,
he sends hopes aloft on the wings
of birds while at his feet nightmares
rumble and churn, climb high until
crater dominates morning-pink sky.

II

Ascension I

That night he made the pilgrimage, his ascent lit
by the slow play of burning light, mounds of cinders
an offering. Half the sky obscured by stars streaking

to oblivion. Extinguished souls filled the black path.
Shards of earth rained down like broken crockery,
the volcano a wavering silhouette behind.

To the east across bottomless pits and petrified flow,
cairns marked a trail to the summit. The crater
painted the clouds with halos of fire.

The trail zigzagged through the wind, the roar
of the volcano, the rumbling of the earth herself.
The earth shook as he walked a low wall

through ragged sky, flanked by lava seething
through slag the color of dried blood,
spewing fountains of flame and rock.

He reached the viewing platform at crater rim.
Below, magma crashed over basalt walls.
In his viewfinder, the inferno was F's gap-toothed smile.

Still growing, fountaining, overflowing, the crater stretched
toward the sea and the living rooms and telephone lines
that fanned out from the shore.

CHORUS

Ah!

It was almost visible: hanging above him
glowing incandescent, a perfect bubble
of inspiration containing one stone, two
birds, and a lashing of fear.

Scar Tissue

He coaxed her to the scene of her combustion,
spread cinders from shore to summit
along lines of silvered lava flow.

Dust spilled into black stone pit,
the slope behind bleached white, sculptural,
broken limbs displayed against ingenuous blue sky.

He poured wine, luxuriating.

On volcano edge, he imagined F with knees drawn up,
all he surveyed charred. Sulfur stained the air.
The wine in his teeth tasted of burning.

She tried to be brave, fingers combing
emptiness. Life followed the path whose walls
bled ferrous red. The creator sacrificed his earth.

In Memoriam

Banana plants flourished
Tall fronds cried out in blue
The last greenhouse
   (Curled glass-bubble banks of scarlet leaves
    Battered ginger a pungent mist)
The mirror marking their claim

Higher up, a surveilling hawk on a pole
A sign read *volcano*
Smothered in fuchsia
A landmark melting into cloud

Lifeless garden held back jungle
Nests of fog and fern
Shadows like ghost ships
With ragged sails

The red stains resembling men were azaleas

(*Stage directions*: Lilies, plumerias, orchids around her body and heaped atop the slick mahogany dripping with yellow beeswax below wreathes of incense and stained light from the glass through which it is viewed.)

CHORUS

One Thousand Ways to Leave Your Lover

And none of them right.

Revelation

His father, half of his world, repaid him not with absence
but with presence, final and absolute.

His shade spoke of home, truth, the sustaining ruthlessness
of each. He wove visions

    of fog-shrouded tree ferns, sand, a fortress of dark lava rift
    twinkling with tremors. Her heartbeat spewing blue cinder tears.

The volcano merely a closet, empty but for its golden crescent
hangers. From the other side came a rumbling, bed banging.
He parted the hangers and opened.
                                      There, F, face bloodied,
eyes glass. He softened, congealed. Eternity filled the room,
her hair a bright channel of water, the hangers
wires and nerves black with blood.

A branch or hand anointed his head, pushing him down,
the weight an echo of thumping heart and tattered rain.
Alone in the volcano, ferns looming, ocean the frame, he gathered
disparate parts, a meaningful whole impossible, wrong.

The caldera face cracked. Terror rising, he willed repossession
of his body, another spirit stepping out of its house
as F rearranged her honeycombed tongue.

He summoned a word.
                              What he produced fell short
with the remoteness of a mechanical limb, an alien brittle limb.

The island was full of nonbelievers turned to stone. Naked
in dreary terrain, crabs scuttling, wind fitful, he watched the glow
of lava swaying, a hungry ghost growing against the dusk.
The bed was a shadow darker than time.

As if to mock him, his father buzzed noisily, landing on his arm
trailing tectonic wisps of steam.

Reincarnation

As he woke, something fell. He crushed it gently,
its pulp the dust of wings on temple stone.

He brushed away its eyes and opened his own
on Greek promises, drunken treachery, moonlight

streaming through storm, a dark silhouette
looming above. He'd read of alien intruders,

victims beyond understanding, interrogated,
probed, deposited in distant bus depots,

hearts mounted sideways. Minds filled
with an absence that haunted thereafter.

Aeneas closed his eyes on the chiseled moon,
a neo-caveman competing with ancient nightmare.

His Apologia

I.

Imagine the emptiness

in the kitchen, the silent stretch
of moments where salt isn't passed
and questions aren't asked
so much as mourned with liquid eyes

or the ocean of once-crisp sheets,
bodies clinging to wrinkled shores

or the pause
between the intake of breath
and the crumpling of skin
around eyes and lips—or the O
of air gulped and expelled
and gulped again

or that feeling in the ribcage
like the grasping ache of something shattered
that never was at all

II.

Imagine, too, her ghost.

III.

Sometimes I think
it's a nightmare. Sometimes I feel
like I'm haunted. They say ghosts
are the ones who couldn't let go.
                Somehow I can't think.

I took it: her hand, the long lines
of fingers twining in mine. Night,
gyrostabilizer awry, sailing into
nothing together. Her eyes
closed on the horizon soon after.

CHORUS

(Bonus Dormitat Homerus)

- That's all.
> The rest of the story
> doesn't mean anything.

>> - You said it would last the whole evening.

> - I didn't like it.

- It's personal. Those strangers, that strange
  affair. That last time, the time he talked…

> - Yes. F blamed the house, fumigated.

>> - Fumigated!

> - In a manner of speaking.

120 Caballero Drive

In his shack by the seaside, Moses smoked
Swisher Sweets, flicking ash onto the floor
with each shake of yellowed fingers,

his living room lit by the flickering of fire
crawling down hills, single malt sweating
at his side. He could see her face forming

in the haze of smoke that extended from cigar
to the volcano above, her mouth open
on translucent Trojans striding forth for war,

cameras held ready. In the neighbors' garden
leaves ignited and for a brief moment the air filled
with the scent of banyans burning alive.

CHORUS

Jubilate Effigio

after Christopher Smart's Jubilate Agno

For we will consider the Trojans.

For they are the servants of the living volcano, duly and daily serving her.
For at the first glance of flame or sun rising, they worship in their way.

For first they steam themselves clean over rifts rending her sides.
For secondly they roll in mud to coat flesh in diamond-hard scales.
For thirdly they sharpen swords upon bone.
For fourthly they flex clawed feet and rasp nails over iron.
For fifthly they coif hair into greasy spiked peaks.
For sixthly they climb mountains higher than birds.
For seventhly they stretch wings to catch smoke, which is the blessing of spirit upon prayer.

For when their devotions are done their labor begins.
For they keep a sacred watch in the spheres against men.
For they counteract darkness with burning eyes and electric skin.
For in their morning orisons they cherish the light and it cherishes them.

For they are of the tribe of Troy, children of magma.
For they are tenacious at the honing of a point.
For they are the quickest to their mark of any creature.
For they are a strange mix of gravity and swagger.
For they regard her as their savior.

For they have been blessed in the variety of their forms.

For they can swim.

For they can climb.
For they can creep, crawl, and scramble.
For they can fly.

Fragments

Midnight, a stone ruin. In the ruin, a shadow
moves across walls: a moonshadow, seeking
shelter. Winged forms circle him, flame-lit Trojans
with bronze-tipped spears. He crawls outside.

Curtains of fiddlehead pines creaking in wind
filter the passage of light into the clearing.
He freezes in parched grass, remembering: *Wait.
It's freezing.   We can warm it up.* He and F

sweating hot oil, the bed melting beneath.
Now, he considers the lost months, the chain
attached to F, the miscalculation, as he slips
past ash-dark ti and plumeria to the shed

at the end of the garden. In splintered windows,
the pinpoint lights of fireflies following his trail
gleam. Framed by the door, F shivers
in sawdust, eyes unseduced, pupil-black, en route

elsewhere. Cobwebbed embryos queued like
abacus beads behind her click, count out
the hours. Chemical fertilizers and hooked iron
tools spill across the floor. Beyond the pines,

somewhere, a siren begins to sound.

Falling

This new-looking woman tugging him across cinders, hot
boulders fellow spirits that flew through Hades stink and steam.

He climbed rippled stone formed of frozen fire.
In the center, a single red fern's vivid slash across gray.

Transient lava hissed from ochrous lips, Nature rearranging life,
staking her claim to crater floor, ash dry land in a tempestuous sea.

Storm winds shifted shattered landscape.

Ahead, F stood on higher ground formed from hot gases,
a high-drama contrast of color against white-capped dome.

He approached cautiously. She screamed.

Sulfur breath shot down his throat. Cavernous vents appeared
on both sides, mouths gaping into the inferno beneath. He paused,

fragile crust under his feet cracking like ice. She an igneous lantern
    waiting
to spark, hair long strands of petrified glass. Iron ore tears in her
    eyes.

He ran fingers through her halo and watched them bleed, knowing
there would be a greater price to pay.

No Casualties

A conversation from extracts of Kurosawa's Dreams

- I can't believe I'm a ghost. I went home.
 I ate the special cakes
 my mother made for me.

 I remember it well.

- But it's a fact. I place the blame
 on the violence of war.

 I survived. You lived
 long enough already. Please go home
 and rest in peace.

 (I know that your suffering was greater.)

CHORUS

Unappeased

She often dreamt of closure.

Star-Taker

after Johannes Kepler's Somnium

He called it a dream but it wasn't—
more a vision, a meld of memory,
science and fear. He sold it anyway:

Himself a small child amongst glaciers,
eye pressed against convex lens,
charting the course of earth around sun

and the magnetic pull of the moon.
His mother a witch, father a mercenary
absence. The boy no stranger to turning tides.

For solace he imagined lunar landscapes,
turned his mind to the mundane earth
only when he felt it shaking beneath him,

when the witch staked out in icy corrie
sang or sobbed too loud to ignore.
He'd never really known her;

he'd known her too well, felt the tendrils
of herbs from her bag twine round his brow,
the prick of bone needles in skin,

the chill of her gaze as he numbered the stars.
He inked her into his maps, the sun a rival
to the flames that circled her,

that licked, caressed, beckoned
so hot parchment singed as he drew.
He couldn't reach her, couldn't risk

singe-mark scars on tender skin,
the chance of hysteric eruption, of slipping
or sliding in the warm melt of glaciers

formed from frozen tears. Instead
he cried with her, felt the burn of salt
on wind-chapped cheeks, hard eyes

of the town holding him back
even as the flood crested at their doors
and threatened to shake shielings loose.

Earth-mother, he sang. Moon-tether,
awash in your tears. Be still the storm,
temper the flame. I wash in your tears.

And still they flowed, gathering force
and gravel, scraps of lumber and old ashes,
dust and debris, a deluge of mud

swallowing everything in its wake.

CHORUS

The Ocean

Marry the ocean, my father, muscles oiled and gleaming.

To capture F on film for all time sandwiched between extremes,
paper masks turn, cast their eyes on desolation. The landscape chills
as the volcano
warms.

Marry the ocean, my father, dip smoking toes in cooling sea.

Night streets smell fertile and damp, an outpost between volcano
and surf, soon to be reclaimed. In this wilderness of gloom
and endless ferns, the journey's end is a single burnt bed.

Marry the ocean, my father, tangle with bright salt and seaweed.

Phosphoric, forgotten ancestors shake with outbursts,
emphatic firecrackers sown as seed. Conflict peppers the air
like the drum of hail on tin roofs.

Marry the ocean, my father. In swift-running water, Trojans
like lava surely harden, slow, and decay.

Adrift

In the Pacific, the misshapen/mistaken/forsaken
/awakened/unshaken (he was uncertain) woman
shrank from his sight:

Her mouth a harbor, teeth
reefs to be avoided with
fragile prow, neon of bars
flickering red and blue
against plate glass in the
hollows of hills where
eyes would be.

Higher up, red
fern and fire wound
round temples, twisted
down to tangle
with the jewel tones of
sunbrellas strung along
her coasts.

He strained to see through the steam
of lava meeting water, to run his eyes
one last time over curves of sand and stone.

Respite

That dream, not so much a dream as a garden
in morning trembling with fine-grained light.

Ferns, orchids, azaleas hung from trees,
colors oil on air, stillness palpable, holy.

In sunlight, F was a flower bent shyly, each petal
a lacy cluster, her breath pollen drifting.

Fine hairs covered the hollows where
pliant leaf met shaded stem, resting places

for crab spiders and the secretions of bees.
He sifted soil through fingers

around her lacework of roots, lifted her tenderly
and placed her in a blue-glazed clay pot.

She brightened his windowsill but then he awoke,
turned, sobered. F was not a flower unclaimed.

Embarrassed, he found himself aimlessly drifting.
The sun bathed in the sea.

CHORUS

The Storm

Well, she called up a storm, didn't she,
a right violent storm. He'll have trouble
getting out of that one, he will.

A Rough Guide to Exile

The corner porthole framed F. He knew her, her spine
a lantern's breath against the dark. A leg, a breast, her ear
luminous. He stepped outside.

Storm seas tossed, water lashing his legs, rain
a keen through torn sails. The *Metaphor* shook
in ash-laden wind.

He dove through rising waves to coral reef
and pried. Jonah underwater, rooting for mollusks.
Her hair whitening with each attack.

At rock-strewn bottom, barnacles cut into callus.
Sharks with Trojan smiles swam close
as rifts blossomed across the ocean floor.

He wrapped himself in seaweed and held air
in his cheeks to help himself float. At dawn
his salt-scoured body washed up on the shore.

The island shuddered, spine reeling into shadow.

III

(*Stage directions*: Set as backdrop
an enlarged vintage travel poster
featuring a hula dancer posed
in triplicate against turquoise sea
and a scattering of pineapples,
hands cradling ukuleles and cocktails
and bundles of jasmine lei
smoldering and crumbling to ash.)

The Late King of the Blues

A lingering spirit, hair tangled
with Estée Lauder trappings,
her face and limbs flaming:

The ghost approached like an ice age.
He thought he'd penned her in for Saturday.
He scraped the crud from his pipe

and dressed to disco, indulging
in depressing kithara music,
a ventriloquist King of the Blues.

CHORUS

I like my words
the way I writ 'em:
graffiti, lush and dark.

Retreat

An army of lava advancing, cinders
crackling underfoot, heads ornate spears
tattooed with moods; the Trojans
crossed the bleached desert of her skull,
feet pounding a rhythm in time to the hiss
of steam venting into the storm.

Her soldiers bore no shields, chests bare
but for funeral leis in blistering heat, skin
a calligraphy of battle and autopsy scars.
They gathered on the edge of grass
withering in their wake, their standard
a red-rimmed eye.

The earth rumbled and the Trojans
marched forward, lovingly-honed blades
tracking his flight. The ring of their conches
echoed through his ears, his eyes pricked
by the steely gaze and poisoned claws
of living shades of fear.

The beat of the steel drums—anarchic, metallic—
meant there was no going back to the volcano.

CHORUS

Great Gwdihŵ Speaks

Descartes considered the angles,
the trajectory of lava and edged stone,
the curve of the road sloping
from crater rim to oil slick lips
to the rock-strewn beach where he sheltered.

It didn't add up: his theories
broken, books singed, neat diagrams
documenting his failures.

I am he thought,
royally screwed if I stay here.
Sweat sizzled on his brow
but plotting a safe course
out from the cinders eluded him.

But do not weep:

We took pity on him. The failed philosopher,
wisdom wisps of half-understood history
muddled with single malt and salt
tears so acidic they scorched the earth.

He mistook our pity for faith,
help for hope. He chose not to hear.
And we didn't disabuse him;
it was better that way.

CHORUS

The Moon

Distant, cold, scattered with remnants
of ancestresses broken back
when his father was the wind and
women were easier to kill.

Rising over the sea, rippled
craters growing from the impact
of intentions hitting far from
home, held in orbit around her.

O, tired hero: look up, up!

Lift Off

Yuri didn't realize the appeal of pajamas
until he decided to fly to the moon:
smoking resins, he contemplated the weightless
float he ached for, gravity-free, unhindered
by boxer briefs, but deadly now.

He regretted his stupid human skin,
pink from burns and puckered with holes
for hair and oils to escape an arrogant system,
for dust and UV radiation to slip in.

He mined closed corner stores
and beauty parlors for swag before he departed,
loomed fruit too earthly, too planet-bound;
armored in lost innocence he might soar.

He stroked a second skin of sticky Gatorade,
laced his boots and buckled his tin helmet
tight. Crouched on the runway, he waited
for the next eruption to launch himself moonward
on the sulfurous updraft.

(*Stage directions*: Linger on the stage—
empty, dark—for long seconds
before fading in tempest rain on tin roofs
and the whining brilliance of
wind and sun through palms and the smell of
green growing things.)

Flight

A legion or more in orbit
as if by invitation, firefly warriors circling
little Icarus plummeting

with impractical wings.
Feathered bodies dropped about him,
his devotees caught in the fire.

He'd happily mistaken for moonlight
the bronze aura of a fury of lovers
grinding hapless men to dust.

Space Junk

The sky pummeled him, slapped him hard
on both cheeks, shook him by the shoulders.
Circling the control tower, he agreed

one could hardly see past the windsuck,
the blue glittering channel of tears, his life
in thrall now to a volcano likely to bury him.

He back-flipped around fleeing birds, divorcees
all of them, singing *His luck was sobering like the look
she'd given when he said 'It's over for us.'* Olé!

Penitent, island-bound, he dropped into the dark
shadow of cloud crowning F's sneering dome.

Ascension II

In the morning, feathers
coated the lawn, the picket fence,
the charred remnant of porch.

She gathered them,
pegged them on clotheslines
to crisp in the sun, ordered by size.

The corners of her eyes itched
as she doused them in petrol
and flicked a match onto the pile.

That night she mixed ash into enamel
and climbed tarred telephone poles
to paint birds back onto the wires.

CHORUS

Logistics

Why the fuck would he ever think
he could make it to the moon?
                    (it's in space)

Descent into Dark Shadow

He touched down at crater rim, taxied to a stop.
Official greeters, bare-armed Trojans with plumeria smiles,
readied him for the descent, cameras in hand.
The scent of drunk spirits filled the air.

The Trojans surrounded Henzeru, removed his leis.
They took a tangled route through Japanese gardens
brimming with banyans, roots varnished by fire.
Their destination: a gaunt silhouette
fronting a small mochi house molding in rain.

Flowerless, naked, unmistaken for faithful,
he looked up to see F.
Where you goin', anyway?

To answer was to admit. Silence filled the volcano.
Clocks ticked, tall and gilded as coffins.

She guided him into the gnarled hollow, returned
with a pot of tea. Exaggerated red eyes stained the shadows,
death nibbling away at the walls. A few tattered souls
hung adrift in the fog.

Inhaling, he admired her ghostly legs, their gradual ascent
to elevation marker unwarped by heat.

The volcano coughed, eruption rattling the saucers.
Sixteen thousand feet, she said. *A geyser, straight up.*
You may want to stop. Oh, you may, yes you may.

Ferns curled languidly, dripping spores into his cup.
He traced with shaking fingers a crude map through warehouses,
cinder fields, the lifeless tin-can town to the sea
and the uncharted rifts beneath.

Did you catch the name of that street?
Dead End.

He drained his cup and stood,
the tea a contract-sealing infusion
of yellow ginger, macadamia, and atomized ancestral stain.

The Departed

In the debris of a roadside bar, sipping
single malt, he sat to read his obituary,
a catalogue of mundane misfortunes:

Painfully romantic
                                      Unwanted lover
Skinny
              Stricken by a communal disease,
                  a passion burning inside

Father dead
                  He a miracle,
                              discarded

He sat back, pushed the paper away.
What did it matter? Heart mute, contaminated
by atoms colliding, Christ didn't want to believe.

TripAdvisor

though he'd seen
a superb volcano
all in all he rated
his time alone with her
a disaster

He followed a banyan root to the ocean,

crossing the beach alongside the ruined runway
to the moon. Silvered swells lifted callused feet
as if he walked on water. Mysterious smells
twinkled silver and gold, the horizon
a dark sea rumbling.
Romance broke on nearby rocks,
dashed to pieces now, waves insistent
with truth: the lava vents could not be avoided.
He braced himself and swam in.

CHORUS

Caveat Emptor

We decided nobody told us; besides, a haunted house
has character. The next buyer won't have to worry
about high-rises. And it's quiet.

The neighbors are orphan Trojan children
crying, cats, graves near the street. They all died
by fire, banyan bark caught in their fingernails.

But never fear: this is ethical. We're moral.

We're not sure we like being this way.
When we were small, we called our first consumer
with a survey, cheerfully: *Yes please. [Box ticked.]*

Thank you sir. We decided then that we lacked.
We learned to trade in structures, to frame
the ubiquitous hero's tale.

Predestined

At the end, his vision soared unexpectedly, climbing
to the cloudless summit that beckoned like a beacon—
young, hot-blooded, rising swollen from the sea
to growl at the sky with bared teeth.
A red and black bird flew over, chores completed
at last. Fern spores drifted in its wake, falling scattered
to seed lava flowing into underground rifts.

 FINIS

EPILOGUE

A Good Map

Topographic, with few roads
and dramatic contours free of billboards,
sugar mills, progress, and poverty.

At the center, two volcanoes.
Cracks and craters on the coast, coves
anchored offshore, ancient temples

flying shadows above.
The mapmaker translates paved trails
into prophecy, a warning in red—

subject to slide and fissure.
Waterfalls, sea arches, sand beaches,
soft borders fade in from blue.

The pulp islands fan open,
a reconstructed world.

AFTERWORD

The poet distils,
but also detects misuses of,
language's power.
                     — Vahni Capildeo

ACKNOWLEDGEMENTS

Love and gratitude go to the editors who included (sometimes early versions of) *Volcano* poems in the following publications: *The Missing Slate, The Istanbul Review, The Fenland Reed, Amaryllis, Elbow Room, Three Drops from a Cauldron, Ink Sweat & Tears, Saw Palm, 1110* and *The Nassau Review.*

Additionally, "Star-Taker" appeared in the anthology *Spectral Lines: Poems about Scientists* (Alternating Current Press, 2019) and "Ascension II" appeared on postcards as part of *Elbow Room*'s limited-edition broadside postcard series in September 2017.

∂∂∂

Many people graciously provided editorial feedback and assistance while I was working on *Volcano*, and otherwise helped to make it a better book. Special thanks go to Meirion Jordan, Julia Webb, and the members of the "Primetime" writing workshop in Wenzhou. Special thanks also go to my editor, Summer, and all the other excellent humans at Unsolicited Press who took a chance on this strange project. Thank you all for your support, your belief in this book, and your work to bring it into being.

ABOUT THE AUTHOR

Following a transient childhood, Elosham came of age in the surreal spaces of the American midwest and west coast, but soon left again. *Volcano* was written and edited during periods residing in the UK, China, Greece, and the USA. Elosham is a Forward Prize (Best Single Poem) nominee and has published poems in a variety of journals around the world.

VOLCANO
Copyright©2019 ELOSHAM VOG
All Rights Reserved
Published by Unsolicited Press
Printed in the United States of America.
First Edition.

All rights reserved. Printed in the United States of America. No part of this book may be used or reproduced in any manner whatsoever without written permission except in the case of brief quotations embodied in critical articles or reviews.

Attention schools and businesses: for discounted copies on large orders, please contact the publisher directly.

For information contact:
Unsolicited Press
Portland, Oregon
www.unsolicitedpress.com
orders@unsolicitedpress.com
619-354-8005

Cover Design: Kathryn Gerhardt
Editor: S.R. Stewart

ISBN: 978-1-950730-14-8

www.ingramcontent.com/pod-product-compliance
Lightning Source LLC
Chambersburg PA
CBHW030130100526
44591CB00009B/589